Group

Brite-Lite™

Booko' Fun

• • • • • • • • • • • •

Creative Nylon Hose Play
Games and Activities for All Ages

by
Glenn Q. Bannerman, Beth B. Gunn,
and Lee Ann B. Konopka

Group
Loveland, Colorado

Group's Brite-Tite™ Book o' Fun

Credits

Authors: Glenn Q. Bannerman, Beth B. Gunn, and Lee Ann B. Konopka
Book Acquisitions Editor: Mike Nappa
Editor: Jody Brolsma
Senior Editor: Lois Keffer
Creative Products Director: Joani Schultz
Copy Editor: Julie Meiklejohn
Art Director: Helen Lannis
Cover Art Director: Liz Howe
Computer Graphic Artist: Randy Kady
Cover Photographer: Craig DeMartino
Illustrator: Lynn Sweat
Production Manager: Ann Marie Gordon

Library of Congress Cataloging-in-Publication Data

Bannerman, Glenn Q., 1927-
    Group's brite-tite book o' fun / by Glenn Q. Bannerman, Beth B.
Gunn, and Lee Ann Konopka:
        p.   cm.
    Includes index.
    ISBN 0-55945-497-0
    1. Games—Design and construction. 2. Hosiery, Nylon. I. Gunn,
Beth B., 1959- . II. Konopka, Lee Ann, 1964- . III. Title.
GV1230.B36   1996
796.2—dc20   96-1045
                                                                           CIP

10 9 8 7 6 5 4 3 2   05 04 03 02 01 99 98 97
Printed in the United States of America.

Table of Contents

Dedication

WE REJOICE AND GIVE THANKS to our families for their willingness to let go and have fun being creative with nylon hose. It's nice to have a research lab in your own home and back yard. We also give thanks to a host of folks who have let us lead them in workshops around the country at recreation centers, family camps, college classes, nursing homes, special populations centers, U.S. military installations, and churches of all denominations.

—Glenn Q. Bannerman, Beth B. Gunn, and Lee Ann B. Konopka

Introduction

WELCOME to the world of off-the-wall creativity, recreation, and fun! In a society flooded with high-tech, battery-powered toys, gadgets, and games, we're excited to introduce you to Brite-Tites™—a simple item that provides endless hours of low-tech, imagination-powered enjoyment.

The idea of using everyday items for crafts and games goes back to the early days of our heritage when our ancestors turned household objects into innovative games and toys. People carved bats from tree limbs, crafted dolls from worn-out socks, sewed dresses from flour- and seed-sacks, whittled toys from scraps of wood, and invented "telephones" using two tin cans and a piece of string. Brite-Tites follow this same idea, teaching us to look for something creative in the ordinary. As you become familiar with the limitless uses of these colorful, multifaceted Brite-Tites, you'll understand exactly what we mean! First, a little background about your Brite-Tites...

Several years ago, Richard "Dick" Porter (former plant manager of a L'eggs hosiery mill in Florence, South Carolina and currently a senior vice president of Sarah Lee Corporation) attended a workshop in which Glenn Bannerman talked about using recycled materials for low- or no-cost recreation. The workshop encouraged people to use their imagination and creativity to dream up fun and challenging activities. The following year, Dick brought a box of flawed nylon hose from his hosiery plant and challenged Glenn and his class to come up with ways to use the surplus hose. On that day a new and exciting avenue of recreation was born. Glenn and his family started inventing games, play equipment, movement and dance exercises, and decorations using the hose. Each time the hose were introduced at an event, more people found new innovations. In 1996 Group Publishing added brightly dyed hose to their new Vacation Bible Ship™ program. Brite-Tites became a smashing success!

This book provides step-by-step instructions on how to make unique Brite-Tite recreation items then guides you through several games using each item. You'll also find ways to use Brite-Tites to help people express themselves through movement and dance. We've even included instructions on how to make beautiful, simple, and colorful decorations for any party or special event. As you try out your Brite-Tites, you'll not only enjoy their simplicity and eye-catching colors, but you'll also have the satisfaction of knowing that you're saving landfill space by recycling a surplus product.

And since each craft, game, and activity has been field-tested, you can be confident that your recreation time will be a success. But don't stop with the ideas in this book—go ahead and experiment to find new, unique ways to use your Brite-Tites. (The authors would love to hear of any amazing discoveries you make!) GO FOR IT!

About Play and Recreation

PLAY IS AS NECESSARY for good mental and physical health as food, work, and sleep. In our efforts to "take life seriously," we often overlook play as a means to relieve stress, boost self-esteem, build community, and strengthen family bonds.

As Glenn and his family travel the country using the nylon hose for recreation and movement, countless lives are touched. The games and activities transcend racial, social, physical, and even language barriers. For example,

● When members of a youth group visited a veteran's hospital, they met an armless veteran whose legs had been amputated just below the knee. A teenage girl slipped Brite-Tites on the man's thighs, picked up the ends of the Brite-Tites, and began moving them in time to the music. The man moved his legs as the girl moved the Brite-Tites, and the two danced as partners, then in a square, and finally in a wagon-wheel formation. Before the group left, the man thanked the kids, saying, "I thought my dancing days were over."

● In Richmond, Virginia, Glenn took Brite-Tites to a group of stroke patients, many of whom were partially paralyzed. He put a Brite-Tite on a man's paralyzed arm and showed the man how to use his good arm to move the injured limb in time to music. The next day, the man's wife asked Glenn for his nylon hose. "My husband loved the activities you did and doesn't believe that my hose will do the same thing."

● A group of missionaries takes Brite-Tites to Russia, where the missionaries can involve the people in activities, dance, and crafts without knowing the language. Other missionary groups take the Brite-Tites to Mexico and other poverty-stricken areas where children have few belongings or toys. Using Brite-Tites, children can make enough toys and games so each child has his or her own.

Through Brite-Tite activities, games, crafts, and movement exercises, families come together, strangers smile at each other, children express their creativity, and lifeless feet begin to dance. Just as play and recreation build up the physical body, the ideas in this book help build the body of Christ. Through nurturing, affirming, and noncompetitive games, your group will live out Paul's words in Ephesians 4:2: "Always be humble, gentle, and patient, accepting each other in love." Use these activities to draw your group together, regardless of age, ability, race, and denomination.

Consider the following guidelines to ensure that your recreation time fulfills its potential for healthier living and relationships:

● Select activities that build community, not tear it down. Choose activities that don't waste food. With millions of people living in poverty, it's inappropriate to use food as a prop that will later be thrown away. Instead, find substitutes for food. For example, rather than using an egg for a toss or relay, use a water balloon in a Brite-Tite (just wait until you read Chapter 5!).

● Encourage and affirm participants in each activity. Don't put people on the spot and embarrass them by making them the target of a joke, skit, game, or story.

● Plan carefully, but be prepared to adapt and be flexible. If your group members come up with an innovation or adaptation to an activity, allow them to experiment with their idea.

● Most of all, have fun! 🌀

Red Flags!

CAUTION: Be sure participants know not to pull the Brite-Tites over their heads or anyone else's. Claustrophobic people can faint when they feel closed in. Also, if someone yanks the Brite-Tite off, the nose and forehead may suffer from "nylon burn." Ouch!

CAUTION: Don't use Brite-Tites to tie people together. It's almost impossible to untie the Brite-Tites once they're twisted and knotted.

CAUTION: Never use Brite-Tites (especially the jump-rope) for a game of Tug of War. Participants can burn their hands and fingers can become stuck in the finger holds.

How to Use This Book

1. Look through it from cover to cover.

2. Choose *one* thing to do.

3. Follow the simple, step-by-step instructions as you read.

4. Always invite others to help work out instructions.

5. Note any changes that help you better understand what to do (and send them to the authors!).

6. Look for this symbol ![symbol] indicating activities adaptable for handicapped, elderly, or disabled groups.

Brite-Tite™ Terminology

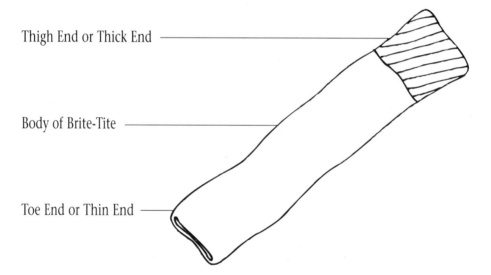

Thigh End or Thick End

Body of Brite-Tite

Toe End or Thin End

(Some Brite-Tites have the same knitting pattern from one end to the other, so there might not be a thick or thin end.)

Since Brite-Tites are made from surplus nylon hose that aren't suitable for processing to sell, you may find that some of your Brite-Tites are different from others. Brite-Tites with runs or stains are still useful for making balls, doughnuts, or rag balls. Be *creative* with what you get!

Section 1:

Brite-Tite™ Games and Equipment

Chapter 1

The Brite-Tite™ Ball and Rocket

Whatever size you choose to make, the Brite-Tite ball is soft, safe, and fun for all ages. And by changing a few simple steps, you can create a Brite-Tite rocket to add a new twist to your activities. So grab a few Brite-Tites...and have a ball!

Creating the Brite-Tite™ Ball

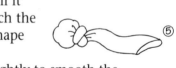

1. Gather white Brite-Tites for stuffing. Use one Brite-Tite for a golf-ball sized ball, five Brite-Tites for a softball size, and eight Brite-Tites for a larger ball.
2. Roll white Brite-Tites into a ball, keeping one end loose.
3. Pull the loose end of the Brite-Tite over the ball to maintain a ball shape.
4. Put this ball into the thin end of a colored Brite-Tite.
5. On the side of the ball where the colored Brite-Tite length continues, tie an overhand knot. Be sure the knot is tight and as close to the ball as possible.
6. Reach into the Brite-Tite, grasp the ball, and pull it through, turning the Brite-Tite inside out. Stretch the outer Brite-Tite so it's taut, and mold the ball shape with hands.
7. Grasp the Brite-Tite close to the ball, and twist tightly to smooth the "skin."
8. Tie an overhand knot firmly against the ball.
9. Repeat previous three steps *five* times.
10. Cut off the excess Brite-Tite to make a ball.

Brite-Tite™ Bonus

To tie an overhand knot, cross two ends of the Brite-Tite, then slip one end through the loop *twice*. This keeps the knot from slipping.

Creating the Brite-Tite™ Rocket

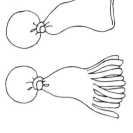

1. Follow the instructions on page 12 to make a Brite-Tite ball, but omit step 10 of the process.
2. The tail may be left as it is, or you may fringe it six inches from the knot and tie on a variety of colorful Brite-Tite pieces to lengthen it. ☉

Games to Play With Brite-Tite™ Balls and Rockets

Bowl 'em Over ♿

Overview: Players try to knock over objects using Brite-Tite balls in this carnival favorite!

Supplies: various sizes of Brite-Tite balls; items such as plastic milk-jugs, tin cans, or blocks

1. Set up lanes by stacking objects such as blocks, tin cans, and empty milk-jugs at one end of your playing area. Items may be stacked in a pyramid or a single row.
2. Make a scratch line by laying a Brite-Tite, jump-rope, or length of masking tape across the floor at least six feet from the stacked items.
3. Have participants stand behind the scratch line and toss balls at the items in an effort to knock down as many as possible.

Variations
● Instead of stacking milk jugs or blocks, set items such as buckets, boxes, or laundry baskets at the end of the lane. Have players toss the balls into the containers to earn different point amounts. You may even want to put toys or individually wrapped candies in each container as prizes.
● Hang plastic hoops at different levels at the end of the tossing lane. Players can toss the ball through the hoops.
● For thematic parties, picnics, or events, paint large sections of cardboard, then cut shapes through which players may throw the Brite-Tite balls. For example, for a Fourth of July picnic, you might design a piece of cardboard to look like an American flag, with several stars cut out for players to toss red, white, and blue Brite-Tite balls through. ☉

Brite-Tite™ Baseball

Overview: This unique twist on the all-American pastime lets teams use soft, safe Brite-Tite balls as they step up to the plate. Batter up!

Supplies: Brite-Tite ball, large plastic bat, rubber bases or masking tape

1. Set up a baseball field in an indoor or outdoor playing area. Use standard rubber bases or mark bases using masking tape. Since Brite-Tite balls don't fly as far as regular baseballs, the bases should only be 45 to 55 feet apart.
2. Form two teams.
3. Give team 2 the Brite-Tite ball, and have this team take the field first.
4. Have a member of team 1 step up to bat, using a large plastic bat.
5. Play the game, using standard rules for baseball.

Variations

● If each team has more than 10 players, add a rule that the outfielders must throw the ball to three players before throwing it to a base. This gets everyone involved and promotes teamwork.

● Play Brite-Tite baseball using a Brite-Tite rocket. If the rocket has a colored tail, call out a color, and have fielders try catching the part of the tail which is that color. ◉

Brite-Tite™ Bonus

Brite-Tite baseball is a great indoor game for a rainy day. The soft Brite-Tite ball is easy to catch and won't damage gymnasium floors or walls. Players don't need mitts since the ball doesn't travel as fast or hard as a regular baseball or softball.

Handball

Overview: This easy game is great for an afternoon at a park or beach.

Supplies: Brite-Tite balls made from five Brite-Tites each

1. Form pairs, and give each pair a Brite-Tite ball. Have partners stand six or seven feet apart.
2. Show partners how to use their hands to bat the ball back and forth. When partners drop or miss the ball, players may move closer together.

Variations

● Gather a group of five to 10 people in a large circle. Have players bat the ball around the circle, in an effort to keep the ball in play as long as possible.

● Use this game as an affirmation. Have the first player say "A" when he or she hits the ball. The next player will say "B" and so on. When a player misses or drops the ball, he or she must say something nice about the last player to hit the ball. The affirmation must start with the letter that the last person said. For example, if the last player said "F," the player who missed the ball might say "Greg is friendly." ☺

Tunnel Ball

Overview: This team game will have players working together as they pass the ball down the line.

Supplies: one Brite-Tite ball (made from eight Brite-Tites) for each team, jump-rope or single Brite-Tite

1. Form teams of eight to 10 players, and have each team line up single file at one end of the playing area. Lay a Brite-Tite or jump-rope at the opposite end of the playing area to form a finish line.
2. Give the first person in each line a large Brite-Tite ball. Say: **In this game, you'll roll the ball through your legs to the player behind you. When the ball reaches the last person in your team, he or she will run to the head of the line and start the process again. If the ball escapes the tunnel of legs, simply pick it up and continue playing. Ready? Go!**
3. Encourage each team to roll the ball gently and to work together to keep the ball in its tunnel of legs. ☺

Kickball Kraze

Overview: This is an active game that encourages players of all ages to be just a little bit silly!

Supplies: Brite-Tite ball (made from eight Brite-Tites)

1. Form two teams, and decide which team will bat first and which will field first. Have the fielding team scatter around the playing area while the batting team lines up behind the first batter.
2. Say: **In this kickball game, you'll get to act a little silly! One of the fielders will roll the ball to the first batter, and the batter will kick the ball. When a fielder catches the ball, the other fielders must line up behind him or her. The fielder who caught the ball will pass it backward over his or her head. The next person will pass the ball backward between his or her legs. Then the next person will pass it over his or her head, and so on. When the last person in line receives the ball, he or she may tag the batter.**
3. Continue: **Meanwhile, after the batter kicks the ball, he or she will skip around the batting team. The batting team will score a run each time the batter skips around the line until he or she is tagged by a member of the fielding team. Ready? Let's play ball!**
4. After three batters have had a turn, have teams switch roles and play again. Play until each person has had a turn at bat.

Variation

● Every inning call out a different way for the batter to travel around the batting team and a new way for the fielders to pass the ball. Batters can hop, tiptoe, walk backward, speed walk, or dance around the line while fielders pass the ball from side to side, from neck to neck, or simply toss it to each other.

Single Rocket Launchers

Overview: This is a challenging toss-and-catch game with Brite-Tite rockets. Individuals try to increase their skills in height and distance.

Supplies: Brite-Tite rockets

1. Give each player a Brite-Tite rocket.
2. Have everyone scatter around the playing area so there's plenty of room between players.
3. Show players how to grasp the tail of the rocket and twirl the ball in a large circle. Release the tail when the ball is in front of your body, so the rocket sails high into the air.
4. Catch the rocket by its tail or ball.
5. Have players toss and catch their rockets.

Variations

● If players use Brite-Tite rockets that have colored tails, call out a color, and have players try catching the part of the tail which is that color.

● Have players challenge themselves to see how high or far they can toss the rockets and still catch them.

● Have all players toss their rockets high in the air then try to catch a different rocket. This game looks like a giant popcorn-popper!

Partner Toss-and-Catch

Overview: As partners move apart, this game becomes more challenging.

Supplies: Brite-Tite rockets

1. Form pairs and give each pair a Brite-Tite rocket.
2. Have partners stand about 10 feet apart facing each other.
3. Instruct partners to toss the rocket back and forth, being sure to catch it by its tail.
4. Have each partner take a step backward each time he or she successfully catches the rocket.
5. As partners move farther apart, have them encourage each other to toss the rockets higher or faster. If you have a large group, instruct the partners on one side of the playing area to toss their rockets at the same time. The partners who are catching the rocket will have a challenging time finding their own rocket among the many soaring through the air!

Orbit the World ♿

Overview: As the Brite-Tite rocket "orbits" the circle, players will get to know each other in a fast-paced game.

Supplies: Brite-Tite rockets

1. Form a circle, and have players introduce themselves.
2. Say: **In this game, you'll try to toss the Brite-Tite rocket as quickly as possible to people who fit the category I call out. Let's start by tossing the Brite-Tite rocket to people wearing red.**
3. Toss the rocket to someone wearing red, and have that person toss the rocket to another person who's wearing red as quickly as possible. Every few seconds, call out a different category of people to toss the rocket to, such as people whose names start with a P, people wearing shoes with laces, or people with blue eyes.
4. If someone throws the ball to a person who doesn't fit into the appropriate category, have those two players trade places in the circle.

Variations

● To liven up the game, add another rocket to the circle. If you add more rockets (up to three), be sure players make eye contact before tossing rockets to each other.

● If you have a large group of 25 or more people, play this game with small groups of five to eight players. After a few rounds, form new groups so people can get to know more members of the larger group. ◉

Rocket Golf

Overview: Brite-Tite rockets take the place of golf equipment for a fun indoor or outdoor game.

Supplies: Brite-Tite rockets; paper; marker; tape; wooden dowels (optional); buckets of various sizes; Hula Hoops; items such as sand, water, leaves, and straw; score cards and pencils (optional)

1. Design a golf course by setting out various sizes of buckets and Hula Hoops to represent "holes." Make the golf course challenging by placing holes atop small hills, underneath trees, or near playground equipment.
2. Tape a sheet of paper to a tree or wooden dowel near each hole, then number each hole.

3. Use a Brite-Tite to mark off a teeing ground approximately 25 yards away from each hole.

4. Place sand, water, straw, leaves, or other obstacles around the golf course. Be creative! (If you're playing inside, sand and water can be placed in small plastic pools.)

5. Start at the teeing ground for hole #1, and try to toss a Brite-Tite rocket into the hole. Write the par number (the number of tosses it took to get the rocket in the hole) near the bottom of the hole #1 sign. Play through the course once to designate the par for each hole.

6. Form groups of no more than four, and give each group member a Brite-Tite rocket.

7. Send groups through the golf course at five-minute intervals. You may want to provide score sheets and pencils so individuals can keep track of the number of tosses it takes to get their rockets in each hole. Groups may want to tally all their scores for a group grand total!

Variations

● If inclement weather keeps you from "golfing" outside, set up a creative course inside your church, a community center, or a local school. Place the holes on tables, under chairs, or atop file cabinets. For added safety make smaller Brite-Tite rockets, and be sure to put away any breakable items.

● Use any combination of Brite-Tite equipment to play through the golf course. ⊙

Chapter 2

Brite-Tite™ Doughnuts

Brite-Tite doughnuts are not edible... but they *are* extremely playable! Once you've mastered the basic doughnut, you're well on your way to creating wonderful, colorful, versatile pieces of equipment. Anyone can make Brite-Tite doughnuts, and everyone will enjoy the games you can play with these innovative items. So push up your sleeves and get ready to roll!

Creating the Brite-Tite™ Doughnut

1. Cut two 1-inch strips from thick elastic Brite-Tite scraps. Set these aside for later use.
2. Pull the thick elastic end of a Brite-Tite up over the elbow of one arm, letting the excess hang from your hand. (Children may find it easier to make doughnuts on their legs rather than their arms.)
3. Fold over the top edge of the Brite-Tite, then roll it down your arm.
4. When the roll reaches your wrist, pull it up your arm and roll it down again. The tighter you pull and roll, the more solid your doughnut will be.
5. When you reach the end of your Brite-Tite, roll the doughnut off your arm.

→ ROLL DOWN

6. Roll the doughnut until the thin end of the Brite-Tite is even all around.
7. Take the strips you cut earlier, and cut them each into two loops to make four strips or ties.
8. Tie the strips around the Brite-Tite doughnut to keep the edge from unrolling.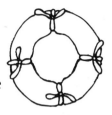

Games to Play With Single Doughnuts

Ring Toss

Overview: In this challenging game, players toss Brite-Tite doughnuts and try to ring a variety of items with them.

Supplies: Brite-Tite doughnuts; masking tape; items to ring, such as chairs, tables, wooden dowels, boxes, buckets, or clothespins

1. Set up your choice of items such as overturned chairs and tables, buckets with clothespins clipped to the edge, or wooden dowels hammered into the ground.

2. Make a scratch line by laying a Brite-Tite, jump-rope, or length of masking tape about six feet from the items.

3. Give each player three Brite-Tite doughnuts.

4. Allow players to stand at the scratch line and toss their doughnuts in an effort to ring them around the items.

Variation

● Instead of setting out items, set out people! Have two or three individuals from your group sit at the end of the tossing lane with their index fingers pointing to the sky. Allow players to try to ring a person. Assign the pointer people silly actions to do when they're ringed, such as singing, "You Are My Sunshine"; running in circles shouting, "The British are coming"; or doing jumping jacks!

Stack 'Em

Overview: Players work together to build a tall tower of Brite-Tite doughnuts as they learn about each other. Then they watch the doughnuts tumble down!

Supplies: Brite-Tite doughnuts, flat surface

1. Form a circle around a flat surface such as a table or overturned box.

2. Give each player several Brite-Tite doughnuts, then say: **Let's see how high we can stack our doughnuts, while we encourage each other. I'll start by placing my doughnut on the table and completing the sentence, "Something I really like about** (name of person on left) **is . . ." We'll continue around the circle, stacking our doughnuts and telling what we like about the people on our left.**

3. Begin the game, and encourage others to think of creative affirmations for those around them. If the tower is still standing when it's your turn again, change the phrase people will say. For example, you might have people name something they're thankful for or describe the most exciting thing that's ever happened to them.

4. When the doughnut tower tumbles, allow the last person who put a doughnut on top to choose the new topic.

Variations

● If members of your group don't know each other well, say the name of someone across the circle when you stack your doughnut. Then have that person stack a doughnut and say someone else's name. Continue, always following the same pattern. The person whose doughnut makes the tower tumble may share something unique about himself or herself.

● This activity is a great visual lesson to demonstrate how affirmation builds people up. After playing a few rounds, you may gather and discuss why affirmation and encouragement are so important. ✪

Human Slingshot

Overview: With a little practice, players will be shooting Brite-Tite doughnuts with great accuracy and speed.

Supplies: Brite-Tite doughnuts; Brite-Tites; items to use as targets, such as buckets, boxes, laundry baskets, or chairs; fun-loving and slightly silly human beings

1. Gather participants at one end of the playing area.
2. Have each participant tie a Brite-Tite into a loop.
3. Say: **Lie on your back with your knees bent and feet on the ground.** Pause while participants follow your instructions.
4. Say: **Now place your Brite-Tite loop around your knees to make a slingshot. Grasp the Brite-Tite loop that's resting just below your knees, and pull it toward you. Place a Brite-Tite doughnut in front of the Brite-Tite, pull back, and let it go!**
5. After individuals have practiced several times, set up targets such as buckets, boxes, laundry baskets, or chairs at the other end of the playing area. Have players shoot their doughnuts at the targets.

Variations
● Form pairs, and have one partner be the slingshot while the other partner stands 10 feet away, holding a bucket or basket as a target. Set a timer for 30 seconds, and see how many doughnuts the target can catch, then have partners switch places and play again. Congratulate the pair that catches the most doughnuts on their excellent teamwork.

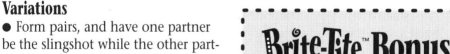

Brite-Tite Bonus

Players may improve their aim and distance by moving their knees out as they release the doughnuts. ✪

● Other categories for human slingshots to compete in include distance, accuracy, height, and the number of doughnuts that can be shot at once.

Rollo Bowl

Overview: This game is great for days when inclement weather keeps you inside.

Supplies: Brite-Tite doughnuts, masking tape

1. Use masking tape to make a 3-foot triangle on the floor at one end of your playing area.
2. Divide the triangle into three sections, and use masking tape to mark each section with a different point-value. Give 10 points for the bottom section, 35 points for the middle section, and 50 points for the top section.

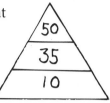

3. Make a scratch line by laying masking tape approximately 20 feet from the triangle. You'll need one triangle and scratch line for every three players.
4. Form trios and give each member three different colored doughnuts.
5. Show players how to roll their doughnuts toward the triangle. Allow each player to keep track of his or her own score.
6. Have players take turns rolling their doughnuts and adding up their scores.

Variation
● To add to the excitement, give each trio a colored doughnut that will be worth double the point value of any section it lands in. Allow each member to roll the special doughnut, along with his or her other three doughnuts.

Dozen-High Relay

Overview: As players stack their doughnuts higher, this relay gets more and more challenging!

Supplies: Brite-Tite doughnuts

1. Form four teams of no more than three players each. If you have more than 12 players in your group, set up two relays at opposite sides of your playing area.
2. Have two teams line up at one end of the room and two teams line up at the opposite end of the room. Explain that teams 1 and 4 will be working together and teams 2 and 3 will be working together.
3. Give each player a Brite-Tite doughnut, and have players balance the doughnuts on their heads.

4. Say: When I say "go," the first person in line for team 1 will walk to team 4, place his or her doughnut on the next person's head, then walk to the end of the line. The next person will walk back to team 1, stack both doughnuts atop the next person's head, and go to the end of the line. As the relay continues, the doughnuts will be stacked higher and higher! If you drop your stack of doughnuts, have a teammate help you stack them back up, and continue. Teams 2 and 3 will be racing too. We'll see which teams finish first. Ready? Go!

TEAM 4   TEAM 1

TEAM 3   TEAM 2

5. Be sure teammates encourage and help each other as the relay slows down and becomes more challenging.

Variation

● If you have a large group and want everyone to work together, have players stack the doughnuts on their fingers or balance them on their hands.

Creating the Flying Disc

1. Arrange six Brite-Tite doughnuts around a central doughnut so all the seams are facing up. You'll need to use doughnuts that haven't yet been tied with Brite-Tite ties. (See illustration below.)
2. Cut six 2-inch sections of a Brite-Tite to make six loops.
3. Stretch the loops, then cut them in half to make 12 ties.
4. Tie the six doughnuts to the center doughnut.
5. Tie the six doughnuts to each other, as shown in the illustration.
6. Finally, tie the outside edge of each doughnut so the seam won't unravel.
7. The ties may be trimmed close to the knot or left long.

Games to Play With the Flying Disc

Corner Spry

Overview: Groups of eight to 10 people use flying discs in this fast-paced relay game.

Supplies: one Brite-Tite flying disc per group

1. Form groups of eight to 10 people.
2. Have players line up side by side in the formation shown below to form a corner.
3. Designate a player to be "It."
4. Instruct It to face the group and toss the disc to the first person on his or her right.
5. Have the person who received the disc toss the disc back to It.
6. It will then toss the disc to the next player (the person standing to the right of the player who first caught the disc), who will return the disc to It.
7. Continue playing until the disc is thrown to the last person in the corner.
8. This player calls "Corner Spry!" and runs to Its position while everyone else moves one position to the right.
9. The new It tosses the disc to the old It, who has run to the right to stand in the first player's position.
10. Continue playing until everyone has had a turn to be It. Play again, but this time encourage players to toss and catch as quickly as possible. Time each team to see who can complete the relay the fastest.

FLYING DISK

Variations

● If you have more than one group, play Corner Spry in a traditional relay fashion with each group trying to complete the game first. The game can also be played using a large geodball (page 32).

● If group members don't know each other well, have It call out each person's name as he or she tosses the flying disc. ◉

Flying-Disc Soccer ◈

Overview: Soccer is easy and fun for everyone, and with the flying disc, it's even easier. This game is easily adapted for people in wheelchairs.

Supplies: one Brite-Tite flying disc, cones or goal markers, soccer field or large playing area

1. Set up two goals on opposite ends of a large playing area. If you're playing inside, use a basketball court, and set up the goals under the basketball net.
2. Form two teams, and have team members scatter across the entire playing area. Each team will need to choose a goalie, who will stand inside the goal area. Remind teams that they'll need to have players near each goal as well as in the middle of the field.
3. Be sure teams know which goal they're defending and which goal they're aiming for, then explain that this game is similar to soccer, except a flying disc will be used. Tell players they must advance the disc by tossing it to another teammate—no one may run with the disc!
4. Toss the flying disc in the air to begin the game. Players may move into position when they don't have the flying disc, but they must plant their feet when they get it.
5. Play until one team has scored three goals, then form new teams and play again.

Variations

● To make the game more challenging and exciting, use more than one flying disc at a time.

● Emphasize teamwork by having players stay in one place during the entire game. Individuals may jump or lean to the side to intercept the flying disc. ◉

Disc-Dash Relay

Overview: Everyone will be dashing to their discs in this tossin' and team-buildin' relay.

Supplies: Brite-Tite flying discs

1. Form teams of five or six people, and have each team line up in a large playing area. Teammates should be approximately 50 feet apart.
2. Give the first person in each line a flying disc.
3. At your signal, have the first person in each team toss the flying disc to the next person in line. *Each person must allow the disc to land before picking it up and tossing it to the next person.*
4. Have players continue tossing the flying disc, until each person has caught it.
5. Congratulate teams for covering the most distance in the shortest amount of time or for simply finishing first.

Variations

● Start with teams of four or five players, then gradually have teams join together to make two teams of 10 or 15. This will create a long line of players.
● Use a playing area that wraps around trees, playground equipment, buildings, or parked cars. Players will have to work hard to get the flying discs to their teammates.

Shootout

Overview: This combination of bowling and target shooting allows players to practice their aim while they affirm each other.

Supplies: Brite-Tite flying disc, six empty two-liter soda containers, table, newsprint, marker, tape

1. Form groups of three to five people.
2. Set up the table at the far end of your playing area. Place the two-liter containers on the table in a triangle formation.
3. Print the following set of rules on a sheet of newsprint, and post the sheet 10 to 20 yards from the table.
   ● **Strike** (all pins are knocked down): Give a group hug.

- **Spare** (some pins are knocked down): Give high fives to members of your group.
- **Side Swiper** (no pins are knocked down): Run to another group, and cheer "Two, four, six, eight! We think you are really great!"

4. Have groups line up 10 to 20 yards from the table. Give the first player in each line a flying disc and allow him or her two chances to toss the disc and knock over the pins.

5. As each person "bowls," encourage group members to follow the rules you've posted. You may select a cheerleader from each group to help rally group members to act out their affirmations.

Brite-Tite™ Bonus

Those Fabulous Flying Discs

Take your flying disc to a park or beach to toss back and forth with friends. You may also use the flying disc in any game that requires a Frisbee or ball, such as Steal the Bacon, Name Juggling (see Chapter 3) and many relays.

Variation

- Rather than setting up the pins in a triangle formation, place them a foot apart on the table. To each pin, tape an index card describing a fun motion such as "Give everyone a high five" or an affirmation such as "Tell two people something you appreciate about them." Players must follow the instructions written on each pin they knock down.

Creating the Small Geodball

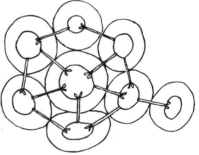

1. You will need one flying disc, a round balloon, and one Brite-Tite doughnut.
2. Use a Brite-Tite strip to tie the doughnut to one of the outer doughnuts on the flying disc. This is your new center doughnut.
3. Tie each of the outer doughnuts to the new center doughnut, just as you did when making the flying disc.
4. Place an uninflated round balloon inside the geodball, then blow it up.
5. When the ball takes shape, tie off the balloon.

Creating the Large Geodball

1. You will need two flying discs and one round balloon.
2. Place two discs together with seams facing each other.
3. Using strips of Brite-Tites, tie the discs together along the outside edge.
4. Place an uninflated round balloon inside the large geodball and blow it up.
5. When the large geodball takes shape, tie the balloon off.

Brite-Tite™ Bonus

For indoor use, use a balloon to help the geodball keep its shape. For outdoor use, stuff a foam ball inside the geodball to keep it nice and round, but soft.

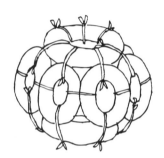

Games to Play With Geodballs

Box Baseball

Overview: This fast-paced game allows everyone to get into the action. The dynamics of box baseball also make it excellent for inter-generational gatherings.

Supplies: three large Brite-Tite geodballs, rubber bases or masking tape, large box or laundry basket

1. Mark off a baseball field on an indoor or outdoor playing area. Use standard rubber bases, or mark bases using masking tape. If children will be participating, shorten the distance between bases.
2. Place a large box or laundry basket behind home plate.
3. Form two teams with eight or more players per team. Teams do not have to be even in number.
4. Send one team to take the field, and have them provide a catcher to remain at

home plate. The rest of the fielders may scatter out around the playing area.

5. Have the batting team number off to create a batting order. Instruct the first three batters to line up side by side to the right of home plate. Give each batter a large geodball.

6. When you give a signal, have the batters throw or kick their geodballs toward the playing field, then start running the bases.

7. The fielding team must work together to retrieve all three geodballs and relay them to the catcher who deposits them into the box. *Remember: Only the catcher can put the geodballs in the box.*

8. When all the balls are in the box, the fielding team will yell "Out!" At that point all runners must stop.

9. Score a run for each batter who crosses home plate before the fielding team calls "Out!"

10. After the batting team has had three turns at bat, have teams trade positions and play again.

Variations

● Use a variety of Brite-Tite equipment, such as Brite-Tite balls, rockets, flying discs, and doughnuts. Each batter may use a different item.

● To involve more players, have the fielding team choose a new catcher for each "at bat." ◎

Foursquare Volleyball

Overview: When you play volleyball on a foursquare court, you create a game that keeps players on their toes!

Supplies: one large geodball, Brite-Tites

1. Prepare a court by laying down masking tape or Brite-Tites to create four 8-foot squares.

2. Form four teams of up to eight players. Send each team to a different square.

3. Have one team begin the game by tossing the geodball to another team.
4. Each team tries to keep the geodball in play (keeping it from touching the ground), with no more than three hits in a row per team. Remind players that they may not catch the ball.
5. When the ball goes out of bounds, the team to the right of the previous servers will serve the geodball to resume play.
6. The team that hit the ball to the team that missed earns 1 point.
7. Play for a predetermined amount of time or until one team earns 7 points.

Variations

● For a more challenging game or for use with a larger group, create the court with four volleyball nets. Set up the nets so they meet in the middle, forming four playing areas.

● When foursquare volleyball becomes easy for your group, add another geodball to your game. ⟲

Zippy Zappers

Overview: This variation of dodgeball is made safe and nonthreatening with a soft geodball.

Supplies: one geodball

1. Form two teams. Instruct team 1 to scatter in the middle of the playing area while team 2 forms a large circle around team 1.
2. Say: **Team 2 will have 30 seconds to "zap" as many players as possible. When I give a signal, members of team 2 will roll the ball across the playing area, trying to tag members of team 1. If you're zapped (tagged with the ball), squat and freeze in place until time is up. Members of team 1 may not move or dodge the ball, but if a member of team 2 fails to zap a player, members of team 1 may move to a new place inside the circle. Ready? Go!**
3. As you watch a clock for 30 seconds, encourage team members to roll or toss the ball gently. When time is up, count the remaining members of team 1. Then have teams trade roles and play again. Congratulate the team that zapped the most players in the allotted time.

Variation

● Allow players in the middle of the circle to pivot on one foot to dodge the ball. You may also allow them to zap the outer team by catching a ball in midair. In that case, the person that tossed the ball must sit down until the next round. ⟲

Stride Ball

Overview: This is an active circle-game for a group of eight to 20 people. Players try to protect their space with quick actions, keeping the geodball from being hit between their legs.

Supplies: one geodball

1. Have players stand in a large circle with their feet spread apart. Players' feet should be touching their neighbors' feet, and players' hands should be on their own knees. This is the stride position.
2. Choose one person to be "It," and have It stand in the center of the circle.
3. Have It place the geodball on the ground then stoop down and swat the ball with his or her open hands, attempting to bat the geodball between a player's legs.
4. Players must keep their hands on their knees until the geodball is batted toward them, then players may bat the geodball back into the circle to keep it from passing between their legs.
5. The geodball must be kept on the ground at all times.
6. If It passes the geodball between a player's legs, that person exchanges places with It. Players may not crouch down or put their knees together to keep the geodball from passing between their legs.

Variations

● To be sure that It isn't stuck in the middle, you may want to set a time limit for being It.
● If you're playing with a group of more than 25 people, use two Its and two geodballs. ⊚

Back-to-Back Relay

Overview: This relay promotes teamwork between partners as they balance a geodball back-to-back.

Supplies: large or small geodballs, chairs

1. Form two teams, and have teammates form pairs. Have teams line up at one end of the playing area, then place a chair opposite each team.
2. Give the first pair in each team a geodball. Have partners stand back to

back, and place the geodball at waist level between them. Partners must lean toward each other slightly to hold onto the ball.

3. On the signal have the first pair in each team walk around the chair and back, balancing the geodball between them. If partners drop the ball, allow them to pick it up and keep playing.
4. When the pair returns to its team, the pair gives the ball to the next pair.
5. Teams may compete against each other or race against the clock.

Variations

● For splashy summer fun, fill the balloon inside the geodball with water. If partners squeeze too close together, they'll get a wet surprise! You'll need several extra filled geodballs if you play this way.
● Partners can carry the geodball standing side by side or facing each other. The ball may be placed at knee- or shoulder-level. ◐

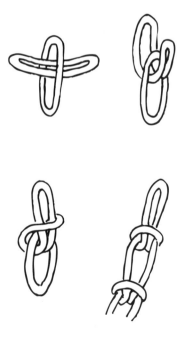

Brite-Tite™ Bonus

Follow these steps to create a durable, colorful jump-rope from Brite-Tite doughnuts! You'll need at least 15 doughnuts for a long jump-rope.
1. As you hold one doughnut, insert another one through it. (See illustration in the margin.)
2. Pull both doughnuts tightly to lock them together.
3. Add as many doughnuts as you want to complete your jump-rope. ◐

Chapter 3

The Rag Ball

Remember pompons and yarn balls? These timeless toys are given new life with Brite-Tites. Rag balls are soft and safe, and they don't bounce, which makes them excellent for players who claim to have two left hands. Grab your scissors and a few Brite-Tites, and create rag balls galore. These items are so easy to make, you'll want to make dozens!

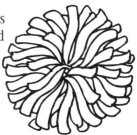

Creating the Rag Ball

1. You'll need a 4×6-inch piece of sturdy cardboard, a pair of *sharp* scissors (Fiskars work very well), and six Brite-Tites in a variety of colors.
2. Cut the thick elastic ends off your Brite-Tites.
3. Use the cardboard as a measuring device to cut five of the Brite-Tites into 4-inch loops.
4. When all five Brite-Tites have been cut, stretch each loop over the 4-inch width of cardboard.
5. When all the loops are stretched on the cardboard, pass the remaining Brite-Tite underneath the loops on one side of the cardboard.

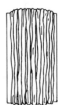

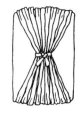

6. Tie this Brite-Tite in an overhand knot, pulling the loops together *as tightly as possible.*
7. Turn the cardboard over and use *sharp* scissors to cut through the loops, directly opposite the knot.
8. After cutting through the last loop, shake the rag ball to fluff it up. 🌀

Games to Play With Rag Balls

Name Juggle

Overview: This is a fun, wild, and crazy way to learn people's names. As the pattern repeats, add more rag balls to create a funny name-game.

Supplies: three or four Brite-Tite rag balls

1. Have players stand in a circle with their hands raised overhead.
2. Give all the rag balls to the person wearing the most blue.
3. Say: **The person wearing the most blue will start our game by loudly calling out the name of someone in the circle, then tossing the rag ball to that person. That person will loudly call out the name of someone else and toss the ball, and so on until everyone has**

Brite-Tite™ Bonus

A Few Tips to Remember About Name Juggling:

● Remind the group that this activity is not a race but an opportunity to work together to catch the objects. Always toss the rag balls underhand.

● Encourage players to make eye contact before they toss the ball. This helps the juggling flow smoothly and gives players a chance to succeed.

● If a player drops the ball, the person tossing to this player must wait to toss a second ball until the dropped ball is started again.

caught the ball one time. You'll be able to tell who hasn't caught the ball by looking for people with their hands in the air. The last person to catch the ball will say the name of the person wearing the most blue and toss the ball to him or her, and the game will start again, always following the same pattern. It's important to remember who you toss the rag ball to, since you'll continue to say that person's name and toss to him or her throughout the game. Ready? Go!

4. After the group has learned the pattern, instruct the person wearing the most blue to add another rag ball to the game.
5. After a minute or two, have him or her add a third rag ball to the game.
6. The person wearing the most blue can take out the rag balls one at a time to conclude the game.

Variations
● Try using a combination of Brite-Tite equipment such as one flying disc, one large geodball, and one small geodball.
● After playing one round, have players trade places and play again, tossing in the same pattern as before. Or, try to reverse your pattern. 🌀

Poison Pass ◆

Overview: This fast-moving, all-inclusive musical game gives individuals an opportunity to act out their penalties.

Supplies: one rag ball, cassette of lively music, cassette player

1. Form a circle, and have players sit down. Give one person a rag ball.
2. Start the music, and instruct the person with the rag ball to pass it clockwise. Have everyone in the circle continue passing the rag ball in time to the music.
3. Stop the music at random. The person holding the rag ball is "caught"!
4. Assign that person an action that uses the rag ball, such as tossing the ball in the air, passing it behind his or her back, or shaking it for three seconds.
5. *From now on,* that person must perform the action *every* time the rag ball comes to him or her.
6. Start the music, and continue the game.
7. Each time a player is caught, add a new action, and have him or her perform all the actions. Here are some examples:
   ● action 1: shaking the rag ball overhead
   ● action 2: action 1 and passing the rag ball under one leg
   ● action 3: actions 1, 2, and passing the rag ball under the other leg
   ● action 4: actions 1, 2, 3, and standing up then sitting down
   ● action 5: actions 1, 2, 3, 4, and passing the rag ball around one's body

Variation

● In an auditorium setting with large groups, many rag balls may be passed at once. As the music plays, participants walk around the room, giving and taking rag balls. When the music stops, those caught with rag balls are directed to
  ● find seven people who like banana pudding,
  ● find four people with the same eye color as theirs,
  ● find 10 people who were born in the same month as they were, or
  ● use the rag ball as a baton and lead people nearby in singing "Row, Row, Row Your Boat." ◉

Parachute Popcorn ◈

Overview: How high can your group pop the rag balls into the air? This is a fun way to get your group working together while having a great time.

Supplies: rag balls, parachute or sheet

1. Form groups of eight to 10, and give each group a parachute or sheet and three or four rag balls.
2. Have players stand around the parachute and hold it at waist level.
3. Toss the rag balls onto the parachute, and have group members bring the parachute down then pull it up quickly to pop the rag balls into the air.
4. Encourage players to work together to see how high their rag balls can pop without popping out of the parachute.

Variations

● Place the rag balls on the parachute, and see how long it takes to pop them off the parachute.
● Place six rag balls on each side of the parachute. Have group members on either side of the parachute try to clear their section in 45 seconds. ◉

Tether Toss

Overview: Rag balls with long tethers are used to adapt ball games for groups in wheelchairs or elderly players who are seated.

Supplies: one rag ball with tether

1. Tie a 6-to 8-foot length of Brite-Tite string (see Chapter 2) to a rag ball.
2. Tie an overhand knot at the other end of the string, leaving a loop large enough to fit over a hand.
3. Seat your group in a circle, and put the tether loop over your hand.
4. Stand in the middle of the circle, and toss the rag ball to a player who will in turn toss it to another player. Allow players to continue tossing the ball back and forth.

5. If the ball is missed and falls to the floor, retrieve the ball by pulling the tether and resuming play. The advantage of the tether is that you can easily retrieve the ball if your group members are unable to reach the floor.

Variation

● Individuals can use tether rag-balls to practice tossing and catching. This is particularly good for people who are wheelchair-bound.

Brite-Tite™ Bonus

Jugglers' Joy

Using three small rag-balls, beginners can learn to juggle without having to chase the balls that drop.

Chapter 4

Brite-Tite™ Rackets

For this one-of-a-kind racket, all you need is a wire coat hanger and two Brite-Tites. This lightweight, flashy racket is great for batting all kinds of items such as tiny Brite-Tite balls, rag balls, balloons, tennis balls, or table tennis balls.

Creating the Brite-Tite™ Racket

1. Stretch the large end of a wire coat hanger into an oval shape.
2. Bend and close the hook of the coat hanger to form a handle.
3. Tie a knot in the toe end of a Brite-Tite.
4. Hold the knot at the handle of the coat hanger, and pull the Brite-Tite over the whole hanger. You may want to press the large end against your stomach as you pull the Brite-Tite over it.
5. Stretch the Brite-Tite until it's taut, then tie an overhand knot at the end of the large part of the hanger.
6. Reach through the Brite-Tite, and pull it back over the hanger to the handle end.
7. Stretch the Brite-Tite until it's taut, then tie a knot at the handle end, and cut off the excess Brite-Tite.
8. To make a padded handle, wrap the extra Brite-Tite around the handle to the desired thickness. Tie it off in a square knot, and cut off any excess.
9. Pull the sides of the racket out until the oval shape re-forms.

Games to Play With the Brite-Tite™ Rackets

Batty Brite-Tites™

Overview: Brite-Tite rackets and balls add style and pizzazz to this simplified version of badminton.

Supplies: Brite-Tites, one Brite-Tite racket per person, Brite-Tite shuttle-cock (See Chapter 1, page 12, to learn how to make a small Brite-Tite ball.)

1. Stretch a Brite-Tite between trees or poles to make a net.
2. Form two teams of about five players each. Have teams stand on opposite sides of the net.
3. Instruct a member of team 1 to begin the game by serving the shuttlecock over the net.
4. Have teams volley the shuttlecock back and forth, using their Brite-Tite rackets.
5. If a team hits the shuttlecock out of bounds or misses it, allowing it to hit the ground, the other team receives a point and serves the next round.

Variations
● To be sure that all players participate, you may only allow players using a certain-colored racket to play for a few seconds. For example, call out, "Blue!" and allow only players using blue rackets to participate, then call a new color (or two new colors).
● Batty Brite-Tites can be played just like foursquare volleyball (see Chapter 3, page 33). Use four volleyball nets, or stretch two Brite-Tites across each other to make four courts. Form four teams and play. ❻

Balloon Paddle

Overview: Any number of players may use their Brite-Tite rackets and a balloon to fan their way to one end of the court and paddle their way back.

Supplies: one Brite-Tite racket and one balloon per person

1. Have players stand at one end of a large room with their Brite-Tite rackets in one hand and their balloons in the other.
2. When you call "go," players will bop their balloons in the air. Players must keep the balloons in the air by fanning them with the rackets as they move to the other end of the room.
3. When players reach the other end of the room, have them turn around and bat their balloons back to the starting line.

Variations
● For large groups, use this activity as a team relay, and have one Brite-Tite racket and balloon per team.
● To make this a wacky and unpredictable game, place a few electric fans around the room and turn them on high. ❻

Blustery Balloons

Overview: Teams try to blow the balloons off their sides of the room in this upbeat game.

Supplies: large balloons, Brite-Tite rackets, masking tape

1. Divide your room in half by placing a masking tape line down the middle. Scatter 15 to 20 large balloons around the room.
2. Form two teams, and have teams sit on opposite sides of the room. Give each player a Brite-Tite racket.
3. Say: **When I give the signal, stay seated, but use your Brite-Tite rackets to fan the balloons to the other side of the room. I'll call time in 30 seconds, and we'll see which team has the most balloons on its side. Ready? Go!**
4. Be sure players stay seated and keep their rackets from their teammates. At the end of several rounds, allow each team to choose a creative way to pop the remaining balloons.

Variation
● Each round, call out a different balloon color that will be worth twice as many points. Teams will try extra hard to keep those balloons from their sides.

Puppet Show

Overview: Brite-Tite rackets aren't just for games. Use them as a fun way to involve everyone in storytelling or skits.

Supplies: construction paper, markers, masking tape, sheet, Bible story or other story script

1. Choose a simple story either from the Bible or a children's storybook. You'll need one Brite-Tite racket for each character in the story.
2. Make a variety of silly-looking eyes, noses, mouths, hair, ears, and even warts! Use masking tape rolls to stick the facial features to the back of the sheet.
3. Choose two volunteers to hold up the sheet so the audience can't see the items taped to the back.
4. Call up one volunteer for each character in your story. Give volunteers each a Brite-Tite racket, and allow them to use the facial features to create puppets representing their characters.
5. While volunteers are designing their puppets, explain that they are going to help you with a professional and dramatic presentation of a story.

6. As you read the story, have the volunteers stand behind the sheet, hold their puppets up, and move them appropriately with the plot of the story.

7. After the story, have volunteers remove the facial features and place them on the sheet again. You can use the same facial features for a variety of stories.

Chapter 5

Single Brite-Tites™

You've seen Brite-Tites turn into everything from jump-ropes to rackets. But what can you do with single Brite-Tites? The possibilities are limitless! If you're out of string, make your own. If you're camping, put your soap in a Brite-Tite, and hang it beside your "sink." If you want to keep onions all season long, put them in a Brite-Tite, tie a knot between the onions, hang them up, and just cut one off when needed. Let your imagination be your guide! Here are a few ideas to help you begin to discover all the handy uses for Brite-Tites.

Games to Play With Single Brite-Tites™

Ski Pole Tag

Overview: This partner-tag game is best when played on a slick floor, using Brite-Tites as your "ski equipment."

Supplies: two Brite-Tites per person, cones, chairs, or other markers

1. Scatter cones or chairs around the room.
2. Show players how to pull the thick elastic ends of their Brite-Tites up over each of their shoes to their ankles to make "ski boots."
3. Have players pull up the toe ends of their Brite-Tites and adjust the tension. Now everyone has "ski poles."
4. Have the "skiers" slide around the floor, weaving in and out of the cones as if they are on a slalom run.
5. Once skiers have adjusted to their ski boots and poles, have them form pairs and choose one partner to be "It."
6. Have partners move 15 to 20 feet apart, depending on the size of your playing area and the number of players.
7. When you say "go," the Its will ski around the room, trying to tag their partners.
8. When It tags his or her partner, have partners trade roles. The new It must count to 10 before skiing after his or her partner.

9. As skiers pursue their partners, caution everyone to avoid bumping other skiers so they
don't cause an avalanche!

Variation

● The leader (or "ski instructor") must watch
the slopes carefully and determine if the Its are
able to catch their partners. If they're having
trouble, the ski instructor can yell
"Snowstorm!" and reverse the roles. ◐

Ski-Slalom Relay

Overview: Here is a relay game that will send your group "schussing" into fun.

Supplies: two Brite-Tites per person; cones, chairs, trash cans, or other
markers

1. Set up a slalom course for each team using chairs, trash cans, cones, or
other markers.
2. Follow steps 2 and 3 from Ski Pole Tag.
3. Form teams of six to eight players per team, and have the teams line up at
one end of the room.
4. On your signal have the first player in each line "ski" the course, zigzag-
ging around the objects. When players reach the other end of the room,
have them zigzag through the course on their way back to their teams.
5. The next player in each line may start the course when the first player
crosses the starting line.
6. Continue until all skiers have completed the course. ◐

Island Mixer   Begin with

Overview: This is an excellent game to help people get to know each other
in a hurry.

Supplies: Brite-Tites, cassette of upbeat music, cassette player

1. Tie the ends of a Brite-Tite together to form a loop. Scatter several loops
on the floor to create "islands." The number of loops you use will depend
on the size of your group.
2. Have players spread out around the room.

3. Start the music, and instruct players to walk around the room without stepping on any islands.
4. After a few seconds, stop the music, and have each player hurry to the nearest island and place one foot inside it.
5. Call out an instruction such as "Find out the first name of everyone on your island" or "Name your island."

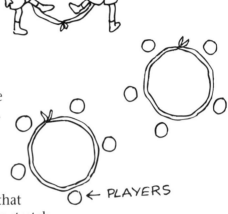

6. After a minute, start the music and remove one or two islands. The next time you stop the music, more people will crowd onto each island. You may want to tell players to help each other find an island.
7. Continue playing until the entire group is on one island. The beauty of playing with a Brite-Tite loop is that the last remaining island can always stretch to include everyone! ◉

← PLAYERS

Indianapolis Speedway

Overview: This game gets players working together to move their Brite-Tite "car" around the racetrack!

Supplies: two Brite-Tites per group

1. Form groups of eight to 10 players. Give each group two Brite-Tites, and show them how to tie the Brite-Tites together with an overhand knot.
2. Have each group tie a second knot eight inches from the end, making a loop with an 8-inch tail. The tail on the loop represents the team car.
3. Instruct each group to give its car a creative sponsor name such as Hershey's, Nike, or Kleenex.

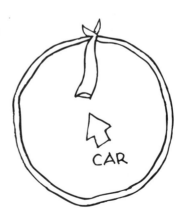

CAR

4. Have each group form a circle (players may be seated or standing), and instruct players to hold onto the Brite-Tite loop, palms down. Have one player act as the starter by holding the car between his or her hands.

5. Call out, "Start your engines!" and have players make car noises. On your signal, have group members pass the car around the racetrack by sliding the Brite-Tite to the right until the car is back between the starter's hands.

6. When the car makes a complete circle, have group members raise their hands and shout, "Finish line!"

7. Teams may race again, trying to better their scores, or they may race against other groups.

Variations

● Challenge your "drivers" by having group members stand with their backs to the middle of the circle and move the car behind their backs.

● Vary the number of laps for each race. 🌀

Brite-Tite™ Loop Pass

Overview: How can a group pass the Brite-Tite loop around the circle while holding hands? This is a great community builder for any size- or age-group.

Supplies: Brite-Tites

1. Tie the ends of a Brite-Tite together to create a loop.

2. Have group members join hands and form a circle.

3. Have two people drop hands, then place the loop between them so their hands are joined through the loop.

4. To begin the game, have the person to the right of the loop pass the loop over his or her body and onto the next person's arm without letting go of the other players' hands.

5. Continue passing the loop until each member of the group has passed the loop over his or her body.

Variations

● Make a loop with two Brite-Tites to make the game a little easier.

● Use two loops, but send them in opposite directions. Have group members guess which loop will make it back to the starting point first.

Water-Balloon Toss ⬥

Overview: This innovative balloon toss does away with the hassle of picking up bits of burst water-balloons.

Supplies: Brite-Tites, balloons, scissors, and water

1. Put an uninflated balloon into the toe end of a Brite-Tite, with the lip of the balloon sticking out.
2. Stretch the open end of the balloon around a faucet or spigot, fill up the balloon, and tie it off.
3. Using an overhand knot, tie the toe end of the Brite-Tite closed, then tie a knot on the other end of the balloon.
4. Use these Brite-Tite balloons in any games that require water balloons. The bright tails that sail behind the water balloons make any game more colorful.
5. When the balloon bursts, cut the Brite-Tite just above the knot. Then use the tail to create another Brite-Tite water balloon. Cleanup is simple because the balloon bits remain inside the Brite-Tite.

Brite-Tite™ Tangle

Overview: Group members work together to untangle their Brite-Tites.

Supplies: one Brite-Tite per person

1. Form a circle, and give each player a Brite-Tite.
2. Say: **Put the Brite-Tite on your right hand so it covers your hand. The rest of the Brite-Tite will hang down. Now reach out with your left hand and grab the end of someone else's Brite-Tite. Be sure you're attached to two different people!**
3. On your signal, have group members untangle their Brite-Tites and form a circle without letting go of their Brite-Tites. Individuals may climb through, over, and under each other.

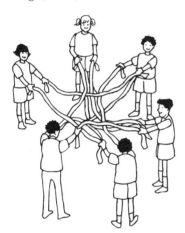

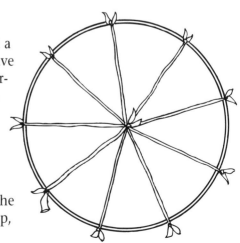

Brite-Tite™ Bonus

It's OK if your group members can't completely untangle their Brite-Tites. If they find themselves at an impasse, simply tell them to let go and try again.

Hoop Weaving

Overview: Players use Brite-Tites and a plastic-hoop frame to weave designs as they share information about themselves.

Supplies: one Hula Hoop, scissors, five Brite-Tites, ½ Brite-Tite per person

1. Tie the toe end of one Brite-Tite to the Hula Hoop, stretch it across the hoop, and tie it to the opposite side.

2. Repeat this process with three more Brite-Tites to create a wagon-wheel design.

3. To form an uneven number of spokes, tie the toe end of the fifth Brite-Tite to the middle section. Stretch it out to an edge, tie it off, and trim the excess near the knot. (An uneven number of spokes is needed to weave a design.)

4. Adjust the spokes so they're evenly spaced around the plastic hoop. Trim any excess Brite-Tite at the edge of your wheel.

5. Have players sit in a circle, holding the hoop parallel to the floor.

6. Have one player begin by tying his or her Brite-Tite half to the center of the wheel then weaving it over and under the spokes.

7. When the first player comes to the end of his or her Brite-Tite, the next person may tie his or her Brite-Tite to the first person's Brite-Tite and continue weaving. Continue until all players have woven their Brite-Tites onto the hoop.

8. As group members weave, have them tell different things about themselves, such as birthday memories, favorite Bible verses, or unusual things about their most recent vacations.

Variations

● Have the first weaver begin a story. When the first weaver runs out of Brite-Tite, have the second weaver continue the story. Allow the last group member to end the story. You may want to set the theme of the story by starting with the phrase "It was a dark and stormy night..." or "Once upon a time, in a galaxy far, far away..." No two stories will ever be alike.

● Make different-sized hoops by purchasing a ½-inch flexible plumbing pipe from a building-supply store. You can cut it to the desired length, insert a 3-inch section of wooden dowel into the ends of the pipe, and make a hoop. Secure the ends with a glue gun or duct tape. 🌀

Section 2:

Brite-Tite™
Celebrations:
Movement, Dance,
and Decorations

Chapter 6

Freestyle Movement

Anyone who's tried to get people excited about movement and dance has heard complaints such as "I've got two left feet," "I'm not holding a *girl's* hand!" or "I'd be too embarrassed." But Brite-Tites make it easy to get people moving to music in a simple, nonthreatening way... before people know it, they're dancing! This chapter will help you expose groups to the fun of music and movement.

Ways to Celebrate With Freestyle Movement

Individual Movement

Overview: Any number of participants can move to music with Brite-Tites on their hands.

Supplies: one Brite-Tite per person, cassette tape of upbeat music, cassette player

1. Distribute Brite-Tites, then say: **Put one hand into the thick end of your Brite-Tite, and pull it up to your wrist. The rest of the Brite-Tite will hang loose.**
2. Start the music, and invite group members to move around the room, performing certain motions that you call out. You might ask the group to
   ● make figure eights in the air,
   ● make large circles overhead,
   ● make large circles down low, or
   ● sweep the floor.
3. You can vary the type and speed of the music so participants have the opportunity to move in different ways.
4. Be sure to reinforce the idea that there are no right or wrong ways to perform these movements. 🌀

Painting Party

Overview: This activity helps people get used to moving with Brite-Tites and starts their creative juices flowing.

Supplies: Brite-Tites, cassette tape of upbeat music, cassette player

1. Distribute Brite-Tites, then say: **Put one hand into the thick end of your Brite-Tite, and pull it up to your wrist. The rest of the Brite-Tite will hang loose.**
2. Start the music, and say: **Let's paint our room and make it bright and beautiful! Use your Brite-Tite as a brush, loaded with any color you'd like. Let's start by painting the ceiling.**
3. After a few seconds, call out another part of the room to "paint," such as the floor, walls, windows, furniture, or doors. You may even call out certain people to paint by telling participants to paint the feet of someone taller than themselves or to paint the knees of someone they don't know.
4. Continue until your room is painted or the song on the cassette ends.

Variation

- Form pairs, and give each pair one Brite-Tite. Have partners place a hand in opposite ends of the Brite-Tite, then call out different brush strokes to use, such as wide, sweeping ones or small, circular ones. Encourage partners to work together to paint with their Brite-Tite "brush."

Partner Movement

Overview: Brite-Tites take away the apprehension of choosing a partner and holding hands. This activity naturally follows those in the "individual movement" section.

Supplies: one Brite-Tite per person, cassette tape of upbeat music, cassette player

1. Distribute Brite-Tites, then say: **Put one hand into the thick end of your Brite-Tite, and pull it up to your wrist. The rest of the Brite-Tite will hang loose.**

2. Start the music, then ask group members to form pairs.

3. Have participants hold the toe end of their partners' Brite-Tites in their free hands, making sure the Brite-Tites are parallel and not crossed.

4. Call out directions such as
   ● raise your right hand,
   ● raise both hands,
   ● raise your left hand,
   ● move hands to your own right,
   ● move hands to your own left,
   ● turn in a circle under your Brite-Tites,
   ● walk forward and back, and
   ● walk forward and shake your Brite-Tites.

5. Once group members respond to your directions, encourage partners to make up their own movements and actions in time to the music.

Variation

● A natural progression is to a game called Mirrors. Have partners face each other and choose one partner in each pair to be the leader. Instruct the leaders to move their Brite-Tites and bodies creatively as their partners mirror their movements. Let each partner have a turn being the leader. 🌀

Chapter 7

Group Brite-Tite™ Dancing

Now that you've got your group motivated to move, it's time to get them dancing! If group members have already worked with a partner, it's simple to slip on a little square dance music and lead them from pairs to large group movement. Wagon wheel, square, folk, and liturgical dancing have never been so easy and fun.

Ways to Celebrate With Group Brite-Tite™ Dancing

Wagon Wheel

Overview: Use Brite-Tites to create an alternative for traditional square dance patterns and figures.

Supplies: one Brite-Tite per person, cassette tape of upbeat music, cassette player

1. Follow steps 1 through 3 from "Partner Movement" (page 57) and form pairs with Brite-Tites.
2. Instruct each pair to join another couple, then have the foursome stand in a square to form a tick-tack-toe square with their Brite-Tites.
3. Say: **Now find another foursome to join your group. Have one group move its tick-tack-toe square over the top of the other square. Your Brite-Tites will form a wagon wheel.** Pause while group members follow your instructions.
4. Say: **Raise your hands to see which twosome has its Brite-Tites on the very top. Those two must trade places by walking underneath all the Brite-Tites**

without letting go of their own Brite-Tites. Then you will all lower your hands. This locks the Brite-Tites together in the middle of the wheel and allows individual spokes to be used as group members move to the music.

5. When each group has formed a wagon wheel, call out different motions and actions just as a square dance caller would. You may call out actions such as

   ● **raise your right hand up, left hand up, right hand down, left hand down.**

   ● **turn, and circle to the left with your right hand up and your left hand down.**

   ● **now the other way back, circle to the right with your left hand up and right hand down.**

   ● **everybody into the middle and shake your Brite-Tites, back right out and shake them down low.**

   ● **all the children** (ladies, men, teenagers, etc.) **dance into the middle, and out you go.**

6. Then say: **I need one volunteer from each group to call the actions. Remember there are no right or wrong motions!**

7. Allow groups to dance through as many songs as you'd like.

Variations

● Wagon wheels can consist of four, six, eight, or 10 participants.

● Liturgical dancing or creative movement in church can easily be adapted to these figures. Groups can choose hymns, praise songs, or psalms and develop their own liturgical folk dances, using the wagon-wheel formation.

● Once groups are comfortable with this style of movement, it's a natural transition to remove the Brite-Tites and have group members join hands. Call out the same actions, and introduce your group to creative folk dance! 🌀

Brite-Tite™ Bonus

Seated Arm-Dancing

There are many situations in which it's not possible for groups to get up and move about. The following activities may be used in auditoriums, nursing homes, hospitals, and other settings in which movement may be limited. 🌀

Alley Cat

Overview: This foot dance is easy to adapt to arm dancing. Individuals move the Brite-Tites on their hands and arms rather than moving their feet.

Supplies: scissors, one Brite-Tite cut in half for each person, cassette tape of "Alley Cat" (or another folk song), cassette player

1. Distribute the Brite-Tites, and show individuals how to pull the Brite-Tites up to their wrists. The excess Brite-Tite should dangle loose.

2. Begin the dance by giving the following directions:
- **Flip the Brite-Tite on your right hand out to the side and back in front of you. Repeat.**
- **Flip the Brite-Tite on your left hand out to the side and back. Repeat.**
- **Flip the Brite-Tite on your right hand over your right shoulder and back. Repeat.**
- **Flip the Brite-Tite on your left hand over your left shoulder and back. Repeat.**
- **Flip the Brite-Tite on your right hand across your body and back. Repeat.**
- **Flip the Brite-Tite on your left hand across your body and back. Repeat.**
- **Flip the Brite-Tite on your right hand straight up into the air and back.**
- **Flip the Brite-Tite on your left hand straight up into the air and back.**
- **Clap your hands in front of your body twice, and pause.**

3. Once you've taught the basic movements, start the music, and have fun! Repeat the dance after the last movement.

4. Be sure to keep calling out the dance directions even when the music has started to remind the group of the movements.

Variation
- After participants have learned the motions and are comfortable with the music, let them make up their own motions for part of the dance. Have the group start with the first four motions, then encourage them to make up their own. End by having the whole group clap twice.

Seated Square Dancing

Overview: By having participants seated and using short Brite-Tites, you can have members of a group of any size dancing right in their seats.

Supplies: one-half of a Brite-Tite per person, cassette tape of upbeat music, cassette player

1. Have participants sit in rows or circles. Distribute Brite-Tites, then say: **Join together by holding one end of your Brite-Tite in your right hand and holding one end of the Brite-Tite of your neighbor to the left in your left hand.**
2. Start the music and "call" a square dance, using phrases such as
   - Circle to the left; just lean to the left.
   - Circle to the right; just lean that way.
   - Everyone dance into the middle; just lean right in, and come on back.
   - Ladies circle to the left; now circle to the right, into the middle, and come on back.
   - Guys circle to the left, and circle to the right, into the middle, and come on back.
   - Ladies circle left, while men circle right; now reverse, and ladies lean right, and men lean left.
   - Everyone raise your hands way up high, now way down low.
   - Raise your right hand, and wave your Brite-Tite 'round and 'round.
   - Now raise your left hand, and wave your hand 'round and 'round.
   - Raise both hands, and clap to the music.
   - Reach out and grab your neighbor's Brite-Tite, and lean to the left.
   - Now lean to the right.
   - Bow to a partner and bow to another.

Variation

- If you've done Alley Cat before this dance, just have participants reach out and grab their neighbors' Brite-Tites and move into the seated dancing.

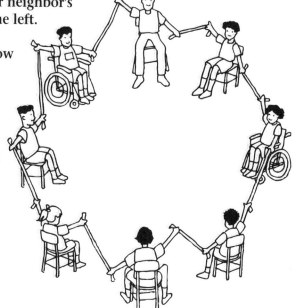

Maypole

This form of Brite-Tite dancing lends itself to special celebrations. In order to accomplish a polished performance, a group needs to practice the movements. You'll need 16 or more players to weave the splendid maypole. Splashy Brite-Tites are a creative twist on traditional ribbons. Gather your dancers, and give it a whirl!

Overview: A group of 16 or more dancers can transform a wagon wheel of Brite-Tites into a fanciful maypole. The colorful "pole" is created as dancers weave the Brite-Tites over and under.

Supplies: four Brite-Tites per person, music cassette tape, cassette player, broom handle or wooden dowel, and scissors

1. Before starting cut the thick elastic ends off the Brite-Tites.
2. Give each dancer four Brite-Tites, and have participants lay their Brite-Tites end to end.
3. Instruct each dancer to tie his or her Brite-Tites together to form one long Brite-Tite. Encourage participants to make the knots as tight as possible and to keep the knot ends short.

Brite-Tite™ Bonus

Since maypole weaving requires at least 64 Brite-Tites, you'll need to order three pounds of Brite-Tites. For information on ordering more Brite-Tites, see page 74.

4. Have dancers form pairs, face their partners, and grasp the end of their partners' Brite-Tites, as in Partner Movement (page 57).
5. Choose one pair, and have partners stand across from each other in an open area while stretching their Brite-Tites across the area. Then choose another pair, and instruct each partner to stand to the right of a partner in the first pair, again having them stretch their Brite-Tites across the area.
6. Repeat step 5 until all partners are placed in the circle and the group has made an extra large wagon wheel.
7. Choose two dancers who are standing next to each other, and have them turn to face each other. Continue counterclockwise, pairing dancers until everyone is facing a partner.

8. Have the dancers with their right shoulders to the center hold their Brite-Tites in their right hands. They'll be known as "Rights." The dancers with their left shoulders to the center should hold their Brite-Tites in their left hands and will be known as "Lefts."

9. To begin the maypole, start the music and have the Lefts raise their Brite-Tites and step forward while the Rights move forward under the raised Brite-Tites.

10. Instruct the Lefts to bring their Brite-Tites down. Then have the Rights raise their Brite-Tites and step forward while the Lefts move forward under the raised Brite-Tites. Go slowly at first, clapping out a steady beat to help the Rights and Lefts move smoothly.

11. Have the dancers continue weaving over and under until the maypole is 8 to 10 inches long.

12. At this point, have a person with a broom handle or dowel move into the middle of the circle and insert the broom handle into the woven pole. This person must remain in the center and raise the pole high as dancers move in to adjust the tension of their Brite-Tites.

13. When the Brite-Tite lengths are too short to weave, have the dancers bow to their partners then bow to the audience to complete the dance.

Variation

● Add a polished finish to your maypole by having all dancers turn to their left and put their Brite-Tites in their right hands. Have them move 16 steps clockwise then turn, place their Brite-Tites

Brite-Tite™ Bonus

When first practicing have the Lefts remain stationary with their left hands raised while the Rights move forward and under. Then have the Rights remain stationary with their right hands raised while the Lefts move forward and under. Have the dancers stop so you can make sure the maypole is beginning to weave itself up (sometimes it will weave in a downward pattern). If the maypole is beginning a downward weave, just put your thumb underneath the pole and push upward.

in their left hands, and move 16 steps counterclockwise. Then have dancers turn and face the middle, walk eight steps forward, then eight steps backward. Dancers then bow to their partners to end the dance.🌀

Chapter 8

Creative Decorations

Looking for low-cost, reusable decorations? All it takes is a little imagination, a few simple supplies, and Brite-Tites to turn an ordinary room into a work of art. You can create lanterns, wreaths, garlands, flowers, and colorful wall-hangings. Braid your hose to use again and again in place of fragile crepe paper. For theme parties, dye Brite-Tites in appropriate colors such as red, green, and white for Christmas; green and white for St. Patrick's Day; and pink, red, and white for Valentine's Day.

Creating Decorations With Brite-Tites™

Lanterns

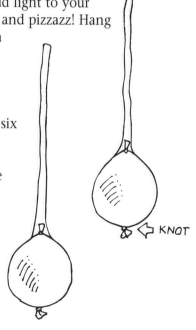

KNOT

Overview: Although these lanterns don't add light to your party, they'll definitely add style and pizzazz! Hang them from a ceiling or trees for a bright and festive decoration.

Supplies: Brite-Tites, 7- or 9-inch round balloons

1. Place an uninflated balloon approximately six inches inside the thick end of a Brite-Tite.
2. Blow up the balloon and tie it off.
3. Tie a knot just under the balloon. Hang the lantern with the balloon end down.

Variation

● If you use white Brite-Tites and colored balloons, the balloons show through the Brite-Tites, giving a nice "glowing" effect.

Garland

Overview: These colorful garlands can be used to decorate borders around doors, stages, or game areas.

Supplies: Brite-Tites, balloons

1. Roll a Brite-Tite into a doughnut (see Chapter 2, page 21), using about ¾ of the Brite-Tite.
2. Take the doughnut off your arm, and place a balloon inside the sleeve of the Brite-Tite. Blow up the balloon, and tie it off.
3. Now unroll a bit of the doughnut, and place a second balloon into this section. Blow up the balloon, and tie it off.
4. Continue this process until the doughnut is totally unrolled. Now you have a section of garland.
5. To give your garland a "beaded" effect, tie a Brite-Tite string (see Chapter 2, page 27) between each balloon.

Variation

● To make a wreath, follow the directions for making a garland, and tie Brite-Tite string between each balloon. Tie the open ends of the garland together to make a circle. Use green and red balloons with white Brite-Tites at Christmastime.🌀

Large Brite-Tite™ Flowers

Overview: These large flowers show up well on walls and ceilings and as centerpieces on buffet tables.

Supplies: Brite-Tites, wire coat hangers, scissors, Brite-Tite rag balls or round balloons

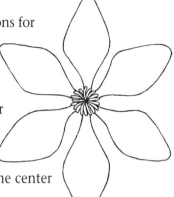

1. Using colored Brite-Tites, follow the directions for making Brite-Tite rackets (see Chapter 4, page 43). You'll need three to six rackets, depending on the flower size you choose to make.
2. Tie the handle ends of the rackets together with wide strips of Brite-Tite string. Bend the "petals" to the desired shape.
3. To cover the handles, tie a rag ball (see Chapter 3, page 37) or round balloon in the center of the flower. 🌀

Brite-Tite™ Flowers

Overview: Groups can create inexpensive appreciation "boutonnieres" for teachers, group leaders, or other group members. Or use these flowers to identify personnel in charge of an event.

Supplies: Brite-Tites, scissors, Brite-Tite string, floral tape (optional)

1. Cut two Brite-Tites six inches from the toe end. Set the remaining Brite-Tite sections aside.
2. Place one 6-inch section of Brite-Tite inside the other with the toe ends together.
3. Stretch and smooth out the pieces.
4. Put one or two 6-inch lengths of Brite-Tite string inside the inner Brite-Tite, near the toe end. The ends of the string should be even with the ends of the Brite-Tites.

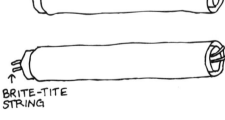

BRITE-TITE STRING

5. Use another length of Brite-Tite string to tie the Brite-Tites together, two inches below the toe ends. Trim the ends of the string close to the knot.

6. Make a stem by covering the tail of the flower with floral tape. Or you can tightly wrap the tail end with Brite-Tite string to make a stem.

Variation
● For larger flowers, use the thick ends of Brite-Tites instead of the toe ends. These larger flowers make great table decorations.

TAPE
TO MAKE
STEM

Plastic Hoop Wheels

Overview: These bright plastic hoops may be hung on trees, walls, or ceilings for an eye-catching decoration.

Supplies: Brite-Tites, Hula Hoop, scissors

1. Use the directions in Chapter 5 (page 52) to prepare a Hula Hoop for weaving.
2. Use single Brite-Tites in a variety of colors, and weave an open "spider web" design onto the spokes of your wheel. Add as many Brite-Tites as you need for your design.
3. Tie the ends of the Brite-Tites to the hoop or to the spokes.

Variation
● Weave in creative items such as feathers, beads, leaves, and raffia to turn your plastic hoop into a special work of art.

Fence Weaving

Overview: Turn ordinary fences into artful masterpieces with Brite-Tites and a little imagination.

Supplies: Brite-Tites, chain-link or picket fence

1. Set out Brite-Tites, and allow participants to weave the Brite-Tites in and out of a chain-link or picket fence to create a design.
2. Brite-Tite ends can be tied to the fence or just wrapped around the fence a couple of times before beginning to weave a design.

Triangle Standards

Overview: These eye-catching decorations are wonderful and colorful for picnics or field-day events. They may be used as directional props or as decorations for any party.

Supplies: Brite-Tites, staple gun, 10-foot 1×2 of soft wood (pine or poplar), hammer, nails, scissors, saw, bucket of rocks (optional)

1. Begin by cutting the wood into a 4-foot section and a 6-foot section.
2. Nail the 4-foot length of wood to the 6-foot length to form a cross.
3. Staple one end of a Brite-Tite onto the outermost left side of the 4-foot length of wood. This is point A.
4. Then stretch the Brite-Tite down to the middle of the longer length of wood, and staple it securely. This is point B.
5. Stretch the Brite-Tite from point B up to the far right side of the 4-foot piece of wood, and staple it. This is point C.
6. Repeat this V pattern with a variety of colored Brite-Tites. The size of your V will be determined by where you staple the Brite-Tites.
7. To finish the triangle, stretch a Brite-Tite from point A to point C, leaving six inches of Brite-Tite hanging from each side. Staple at points A and C.
8. Cut the excess Brite-Tites into strips to create tassels.
9. Set triangle standards in shallow holes or buckets of rocks to keep them standing.

Variation

● To make diamond standards, nail equal lengths of wood together in the middle to form an X. Starting at point A, staple the Brite-Tite, and continue stretching and stapling at each end (points B, C, and D) then back to point A. Add more Brite-Tites toward the center of the diamond.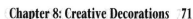

Section 3:

Now That You Know, Where Do You Go?

Chapter 9

More and More Brite-Tites™

Now that you've discovered some of the fun and innovative ways to use Brite-Tites, you'll want to use them in recreation, retreats, large group gatherings, children's ministry, service projects and more. The information in this section will help you order more Brite-Tites, give tips for dyeing white Brite-Tites, and provide resources with even more ideas for using Brite-Tites.

How to Get More Brite-Tites™

To receive a box of over 40 clean, colorful Brite-Tites, contact Group Publishing, Inc., P.O. Box 485, Loveland, CO 80539, or call 800-447-1070.

You can also get a large box of unprocessed waste nylon hose by contacting Sara Lee Hosiery-L'eggs Products, P.O. Box 719, Marion, SC 29571.

To See Brite-Tites™ in Action

Bannerman Family Celebration Services, Inc. has created a video in which Glenn Bannerman demonstrates many of the crafts and activities in this book—plus several more! If you want to show a group of teachers, camp counselors, or group leaders the amazing versatility and creativity of Brite-Tites, send a check or money order for $29.95 plus $2.50 for shipping and handling ($32.45 total) per video to Celebration Services, Inc., Box 399, Montreat, NC 28757.

To Use Brite-Tites™ in Your Children's Worship Time

Children love the splashy colors and stretchy feel of Brite-Tites. So when you put upbeat worship songs, simple motions, and Brite-Tites together you come up with a dynamic, active, and meaningful worship experience for kids! Group's *Sing & Play* music video, used in Group's Vacation Bible Ship™, leads kids step by step through easy motions to some of their favorite praise songs using Brite-Tites. To see your kids jump, shout, dance, and sing with enthusiasm, contact Group Publishing, Inc., Box 481, Loveland, CO 80539.

Dyeing Your Own Brite-Tites™

You already have a can of colorful Brite-Tites...but you can dye your Brite-Tites any color you'd like. All you need is a washing machine, Brite-Tite net bags (for washing nylon hose), and fabric dye.

1. Fill a washing machine to medium level with hot water.
2. Add two boxes of dye. (Open the boxes inside the washing machine.)
3. Place four nylon bags filled with 50 to 60 Brite-Tites each into the washer. *Tie the bags tightly.*
4. Let the washer agitate for 10 minutes, then stop the machine.
5. Let the Brite-Tites soak for one to two hours, then turn the machine to the spin cycle to spin out the water. Run the spin cycle twice.
6. Place the bags in a dryer, and allow it to run for an hour. If you don't put the Brite-Tites in a nylon bag, the Brite-Tites will form a knotted ball! Be sure the Brite-Tites are dry before taking them out of the dryer.
7. Run a full cycle of fresh water through your washing machine, and wipe down the lid and rim before using the machine for your regular laundry. 🌀

Brite-Tite™ Bonus

You can also dye your Brite-Tites in large plastic tubs or garbage cans. Then hang them on a clothes line to dry!

Your New Ideas

Everyone seems to come up with new uses for Brite-Tites. If you've come across an innovation for Brite-Tites, we'd love to hear it! Please include the age group you've used this idea with and any variations on your activity.

Mail your idea to:
Group Publishing, Inc., Attn: Jody Brolsma
Box 481
Loveland, CO 80539

Index

Activities

How to Make a...

Glenn Q. Bannerman B.S., MRE is the president of Bannerman Family Celebration Services in Montreat, North Carolina. For 31 years Glenn served as Professor of Recreation and Outdoor Education at the Presbyterian School of Christian Education in Richmond, Virginia. He is active in the area of recreation and conducts leadership training events throughout the United States and abroad.

Lee Ann Bannerman Konopka B.S. graduated from Appalachian State University with a degree in Recreation Program Management. However, long before college Lee Ann traveled with her father, leading recreation and dance. She is currently the director of a senior center for the Black Mountain Recreation and Parks Department in North Carolina and continues to lead recreation for a variety of groups.

Beth Bannerman Gunn B.S. has been a free-lance recreation specialist for over 15 years. Beth graduated with honors from North Carolina State University with a degree in Recreation Resources Administration. Beth's experience ranges from church leadership, Girl Scouts, and arts councils to directing summer day camps and planning for church youth conferences which serve over 6,000 young people each summer.

Evaluation of *Group's Brite-Tite*™ *Book o' Fun*

Please help Group Publishing, Inc., continue to provide innovative and usable resources for ministry by taking a moment to fill out and send us this evaluation. Thanks!

● ● ●

1. As a whole, this book has been (circle one):

Not much help   Very helpful

1   2   3   4   5   6   7   8   9   10

2. The things I liked best about this book were:

3. This book could be improved by:

4. One thing I'll do differently because of this book is:

5. Optional Information:

Name _____

Street Address _____

City _____ State _____ Zip _____

Phone Number _____ Date _____